Where Land
Is Indistinguishable
from Sea

Also by Helena Mesa

Horse Dance Underwater

Mentor and Muse: Essays from Poets to Poets
(Anthology co-edited with Blas Falconer
and Beth Martinelli)

Where Land
Is Indistinguishable
from Sea

Helena Mesa

Terrapin Books

Terrapin Books
4 Midvale Avenue
West Caldwell, NJ 07006

www.terrapinbooks.com

ISBN: 978-1-947896-67-3
Library of Congress Control Number: 2023939720

First Edition

Cover art by Jorge Mayet
Demasiado tiempo sin que tu estés (2009)
Metal structure: paper mache, wood, wire, textile,
recycled paper, and acrylics
170 x 60 x 60 cm / 66.9 x 23.6 x 23.6 in
Courtesy of Jorge Mayet Studio and Richard Taittinger Gallery

Cover Design by Diane Lockward

for Laurie

for my mother

for those who love across a great distance

Contents

"The night isn't dark; the world is dark.
Stay with me a little longer."
—Louise Glück

"But the words are shadows and you cannot hear me."
—Eavan Boland

Love Letter to a Stranger, with Rain

Years ago, I read of an accident
in a country far from our own.
The medics arrived late, and as the ambulance
pulled from the curb, the crowd sang,
together, strangers making song
of an end we fear. I'm saying this wrong.
Why wait for the sirens?
Why not sing like that now?

This morning, a stillness—
miles and miles of trees. Tell me
how to reach you—which road do I take,
which swimming hole will invite us
where the spring feeds from beneath
and cools our feet? When rain fell
on the tin roof yesterday, I thought
I was in another country, the light
more aged than yellow.
And along one road, a swallowtail,
its ice-blue wings closing like a door.

I.

Late

No one knows you,
the guests already clustered,
their backs all charmeuse
dipping low. Their chatter's
not unfamiliar
though the words miss
vowels, the sentences verbs.
The room's design
you recognize—bookcase,
chairs, not the chandelier.
Barefoot on the couch,
you drum the leather, calling
a stray cat to fill the space.
Instead, waiters offer
cocktail forks on silver trays.
You ask for a dictionary.
When you speak, the words
seep reds, a horizon
behind you. The guests turn
and comment
how hard it is to hear
from such distance.

A Conversation

She's sitting beside me,
staring at the red light. Palm trees sway —
a summer wind I can't feel
inside the sealed car, my thighs sticking
despite the AC. *It doesn't work,*
she says from the driver's seat. Her gaze
a steady line, straighter than the city's grid,
than a row of burial plots. Against
the steering wheel her tap-tap-tap, though
we both fear the upcoming traffic.
For now the perpendicular street's empty.
I watch the red light. *Two women,*
she's saying a year before her sister will bury
her wife, minutes after I name a woman
again. The stoplight's more orange than red —
the bulb wrong; it refuses to change
or wave my mother through.

On Love

For nights, I woke, heard
wings fluttering, circling,
the beat-beat of wings—

for nights, it scratched
the door, animal in need
of an *us*, and my lover

asleep beside me. All
because of a call:
a bat's in my house —

little brown bat
lounging in the sink,
brown bat with little

jagged teeth, its hiss
sharp and electric, staticky
hiss, crackling hiss,

its warning more fearful
than fierce. I cupped
its hunched back, wedged

a mitten under its belly,
and raised it up and out
at arm's length, ditching

that brown bat
on a blue towel under
the brush—and now, it returns.

For nights, phantom of a bat
swooping, hearing what
I cannot, hearing where

I rest, its cochlea shaped
like a heart. Bulbous thing,
ancient thing, let me hear

what you hear, let me hear
the space between us
in this room, this house,

and know this air, these bricks
and rooms are not an altar
built for sacrifice.

If I call out, let me hear
space collapse, my own
cochlear thump, echoing

echoing, song for my heart.

Departure

The last supper, the aroma of the dish, the meat's texture
as she chewed—that isn't mine to know.

If the plane fluttered, if she wept for her own mother
when she saw her new coast. Did she ask the stranger

seated beside her how long they'd visit
as if on vacation? Holding papers, a suitcase,

she waited in line with the others—this I know.
In her favorite dress—perhaps.

Her father's watch left behind—yes.
Her sister, too—yes.

Thirsty, my mother took the fruit
a stranger offered, bit the waxy skin

she couldn't swallow,
the pulp browning in her hand.

Two Variations on Distance

1.

In one hand, the peeled orange,
its pith webbing each wedge.

Her thumb kneads the center,
gently loosens the segments

until citrus scents the cabin
around them. She offers one

to the silent stranger
sitting beside her in 6A.

2.

Perhaps the distance between
rind and center

is a scale—for hand and sleeve,
aisle and seat,

or for two strangers departing
a small plane—

one heads north, the other
looks back again.

Against Paradise

I did not ask to be an Eden. I asked
for someone to tend grasses, prune the wild trees
so branches might rise like wings, their woozy fruit
staining his palms, and so ants and wasps
might teach desire. No brooks burbled,
but some nights, when the birds slept, I heard
waves from afar, and the creak of palms
sounded like the sky humming, each note
sweeping the stars. I'd already named the flies
and the deer uprooting the cassava near the stone gates
before he arrived. Like a cuckoo, he mimicked
birds drunk on berries, stuttering. He thought
seeds hitting the leaves were a gentle rain.
Stupid child, he thought he owned
those first sounds, first words—all he went on
to name, as if all this were for the taking.

The Body Is Not a Stone

In Caravaggio's vision of the sacrifice,
the boy's chest gleams, bare as the knife's tip
and solid blade held by his father
to the neck and cheek. This morning
before the sun rises, I read
about the election. Shadows quicken
in the leafless trees, the walls brightening
from passing headlights. My beloved
asleep beside me. She turns and
murmurs as the sheet slips down
her torso, exposing the knots of spine.

As a child, I learned to fear
what I couldn't understand—a storm
with the power to illuminate
a field, or the way lightning can split
a tree in two. God blessed Abraham.
But one night the boy awakens,
braces against the oncoming touch
of his father's hand like lightning
coming toward him to set the bed aflame.

Recess

The schoolyard scabbed with tar that stuck
to our soles, the sky an upturned bowl
that hung over us, our bodies tired
of stiff seats, of *sit still, sing louder, silence,*
the nuns always watching but deaf
when our backs turned, boys and girls hissing,
Eddie smella, off Orihuela. His Spanish name,
his dark hair and eyes, his gapped front teeth—
all just like me. I hated the chorus of kids
taunting *kiss her,* the boy chasing me
toward the chain-link fence, their *kiss Bucky*
insistent, his lips stinging like a bee,
my *no,* their laughter. Who else could kiss me,
an ugly girl, who else could he kiss but me?

Get Down

Wedged under vinyl, I think only
of the scruff of dirty carpet, seats overhead
like a broken awning, and face
a crouched woman weeping
into her tote bag. I fear what might come
before I rise, run to the back gate,
our bodies pushing through the jetway,
refusing to halt until our feet
meet the tarmac, the crowd of us,
stunned like the child, her pigtails
shaking—*here? here?*

Duende with Poppies

Orange heads atop too-thin necks,
crepe petals I want to pluck and eat, their orange
a sherbet, a mango skin I want to split
to suck the seed, its juice running down my arms.

Rothko orange, neon orange, orange I'd wear
in deep summer,
                    orange the sunlight would be
if given a choice. A chorus of baritones,
a few tambourines.

Orange cardigan my sister wore, lounging
in my dream last night, her hand trailing
the petals—she sang the song we all sang
as children before we knew what the Spanish
meant—such joy for a man dying in war!
                                 If a field
covered the entrance to the underworld, its grass
would be orange—this orange, the orange of street cones
blocking unfinished roads—the same orange
hunters wear to announce they exist.
                            DEFCON orange,
fleeting orange
                 that the breeze peels back
to a merlot heart that clenches, releases,
before the blossom flutters shut.

After Paradise

after Masaccio's Expulsion from the Garden of Eden

Of all there is, you see the couple
depart together. See an angel soldier them out,
sword raised. Their bare feet crossing
compacted sand—the desert calls

as Paradise mourns. The gate's edge
a shore you will never reach, its unseen
garden more fertile than your clay earth,
your tomato plants that branch

small hard fruit. See Adam's hidden face,
the scoliosis of your own back. See Hessian hills,
the color of your grief. The sky dirty
with sand. The air clogged with sand. The sand

that must be in their hair. Their eyes. Under
her breasts. You know they already left it
behind—the rolling light that feeds
every living thing. See ropey shadows

binding their heels to their past. And Eve,
see how her face is leather, already aging
in your world, a world that will never
let them go or give them back.

Our Bodies Stood Like Houses

Dear friend, we wanted it—
the rain—before *too much*,
before sweeping steps,
porches, the water flooding
the street and yard, cars
overturned like bowls.

We were close
then. Loveless and
calloused, you said, enough
to hold back loss.

Old friend, my hands ache,
the grip too tight.

It would be better
to let the water in.

II.

There

Havana, Cuba

No, there, the logistics of marking a place, as if naming
it were remembering—movie theater, ice cream shop,
barber shop; *there, we used to throw snow cones at the
barber, and one day he chased us*; or the distance
between two places—*back there*, that street corner,
that time, and then: *Still there, the barber's still there*.

Or settling an argument—*So there*, hands palming
hips, as if the street name matters, be it the name of a
young girl or a saint, the difference between saying a
church was destroyed by hungry people throwing
rocks through the windows, or by the birds that
came after, nesting and shitting on the altar.

There, I've said it, except she says, *My father's buried
there*, followed with a *somewhere over there*, the word
hollow, a bell half-rung, for which no walking between
stone rows could find his unmarked grave over there.

Catalog of Unasked Questions

How far before home
receded beyond the horizon?
(54 km) How far before *It's too late
to turn back*? (22 km) Before you
awoke, thought you heard roosters
jumpstart the city, only to hear dawn
arrive in an ore car? (1937 km)
How far before autumn
knotted your arms in a
snowstorm? (another 1171)
And slipped on black ice? (9 km)
How far before calculations
became errands or absence?
(4 years and 9 months) How far
before your skin longed
for sea salt, your back for sand
warming your muscles? (the first
daughter) Before you forgot
the taste of fresh papayas?
(never) How far before you cried
you'd never return? (that
was a lie) How far before the ocean
became an unscalable wall?
(90 km) And how far
before the distance
no longer felt distant?
(   )

The Exile, from the Window

Mi niña, you circle the lawn, skip-trotting,
fingers hooked on imaginary reins, half-fisted
the way you once gripped my own fingers.

The snow never ends. You ride out to rescue
survivors, then warm them, heal them
in your refuge. Already I see myself in you—

you know what loss can do. Sometimes
out shopping, the crowd and groceries
too much, I stand at the magazine rack

while the eggs sweat, meat thaws, and focus
on the glossy covers. Everyone I've ever known
lives so far, their embrace now a trace of

something wondrous. The brush of their hands
across shoulders, along my back,
now a long-dry snowfall. How can I explain—

after so many cold years, I'll do anything
to be held, be loved, even leave you behind.

Lot's Daughter

What choice did we have but to flee
the embers falling on wheat fields
burning behind us. Cattle and horses
bolted ahead, their hooves a clamor.
When my steps slowed, my mother
gripped my arm and warned, *Forward.*
Ash salted the unforgiving sky,
its taste bitter on our tongues.
My shoulders ached to turn back—
just that morning she'd kneaded bread.
I'd cut guava near the stove.
Tea steeped. Wild herbs laced
the garden. Didn't we all want
one last glimpse before crossing
that bloomless desert? Her head turned
slightly, and before I could speak,
the rings slipped from where
her hands once were—her shape
like stone before her grains flew.

The want for faith

appears briefly, unexpectedly,
when stitching a loose button
on a new shirt, when watching
the news of another boy shot, when
sitting at home during the funeral
you couldn't attend, and when
it comes, it comes like wading
in the ocean, seagrass grazing
your leg—*Is it a silverfish?*
Stingray?—though it's gone
when you reach for it; or like stillness
befalling a forest so briefly
you don't recognize it until
the chatter returns; or like catching
a movement that startles, shifts
your body sideways to glimpse
what might be the blurred edge
of a dog chasing a hare
or nothing at all.

For the First Girl I Loved

I lived across the street—across two streets.
The cemetery lay behind you, a field of stories

stretched behind a thin row of trees: there
this silence would mean a louder silence,

the sinking of stones, roots tracing their fists,
knuckling the soil. Someone could hover,

talk seemingly to no one—words meant
for someone else. You loved stories of

the past—pioneer girls doing the right thing
in flower nightgowns, a sister saved, a white lie

righted, and you always fell asleep to
whatever hands I whispered were reaching

through the window, the lie you never needed
to forgive. In the morning, you made instruments

for whatever surgery I imagined—a doll's arm
scratched my stomach; a plastic fork

raked my shoulder, then spread salves.
Your fingers trailed the soft fold

of my elbow—skin and head
tingling, and then, a stillness

so unexpected I begged you not to stop.
And when the V of your collar dipped low,

the pink tip of your scar appeared
swollen, raised. I willed myself

not to finger the ridge
stitching your cracked chest shut.

The Lesson

She said, *He is everywhere,*
even inside you. I felt
my bones bow, my organs
crowd with words.
The thin black dog
leaning against a white fence,
the seamstress pricking
her finger, my father sleeping
at the end of the pew—
inside us all, He listened,
a black phone with a stiff dial
connecting one mind
to the next. I listened to
the circuits of my body
jam with sounds, then
a stillness I feared.
Eve left the garden,
she said, *Eve disobeyed*
and He marched her
through gates leading
nowhere, and nowhere
stretches. He knew
before she covered
herself in leaves, before
the core swarmed with bees.
He lived inside her
and felt the thought form.

Self-Portrait with a Cubano de Paso

The horse would carry me away —
middle of the night, bareback, mane wild
with speed. Somehow, there was always
a reason to run — through forests, back fields —
and old shacks to hide in, the straw ready,
feed spilling over. This was the story.
Some days, the horse raced along a back road
parallel to my own. Other days, it appeared
huffing at my window. I wanted that horse
the way others wanted love to bow its head.
It could be mine, it didn't live that far,
just beyond the glass pane and line of firs —
a gentle call could summon it — although
if it ever came, I'd still walk alone.

Reunion

In that airport, entrance doors letting in exhaust,
strangers and shouts —*hija, over here!*—
and more bodies, and from behind the barriers
between us and international arrivals, I search
between elbows and hips, looking for a
posture, something familiar beyond doors
bumping shut, their sighs as they release carts
and suitcases, a wrist, a swatch of linen,
before my aunt's *there she is,* and my *where?*

before my aunt pointed to a mother with fresh hair—
tight curls framing a face I did not recognize.
The distance like my refusal to speak, stubborn
in that Miami heat. Humidity hanging
between us before words could reveal longing.
Already I was losing her. And she me.
And just like that, the moment passed,
her arms pressing my ribs too hard, lifting me
into sunscreen and sweat and light.

The Past

When she dipped into the forgotten
and splayed it across you
like a handful of black paint,
you scolded her for making a mess
of the house. She laughed,
buck teeth flashing. She brushed
your hair, seaweed and brine
on her breath. When someone new
rested her head on your lap,
she sang dirges for those
who'd come before. Some days
she tarried too long. Others
she whistled as you weeded.
She slipped love notes in drawers,
scribbled cursive in cookbooks,
hid photos—your fingers reached
for a dish and brushed childhood
dressed in knee-highs.
One morning, she disappeared.
You swore she'd return to tell you,
the promise harmless
until the remaining details
became the story.

III.

609 Delicias, La Víbora, La Habana, Cuba

Strangers to the house, the house even stranger to us, we crowd the living room I've only seen in a black and white photo. *We don't have much*, the woman had said when we knocked, then opened the partitioned door. Walls in need of plaster and paint. Shutters open, windows grated, ironwork rusty. Of all my mother left behind, only a chair remains, its back missing, its arms speckled with candle wax and yellow paint. I study the navy cushion restitched lime green as if my mother sat there, fussing as her mother trimmed her bangs. My mother shakes her head—*I don't remember*—then she lingers—*perhaps*.

The Visit

What did you expect?
she never asked. And I never said,
I imagine you came home

after your father's burial
and stood barefoot on these tiles
wishing they were cold enough
after the long walk home.

Across this city, arches invite us
into rooms and halls that once stood.
Just yesterday, a street name

forgotten, one she knew
intimately, like her hand
pointing — *there* — like her
father's hand — *yes, there.*

A tree grows in the center
of one house like a beam,
pushes out windows and eaves

as it remembers the sky's promise.
Each branch spreads beyond
walls to seize the space
that's as lost to her

as it always was to me.
She wonders how we could know
a place when there's little left

to recollect. I wonder
how to know her
when there's little left
that we would say.

Ineffable

Tumble of sounds. Her words
like a bird call, its final syllable
hovering. If I could, I would

pull an egg from her open mouth,
so her mouth could mouth mine,
meaning her mouth could say
she understands my thirst.

I would shape her loud palms
into arrows, pointing toward
yesterday, toward midnight

and the silence of her sleeping,
the house sleeping, and the sleepy
darkness I thought was a death cave
through which I nightly crawled.

If I could, I would scrub the words
in the kitchen sink, clip them
on a clothesline, or tumble

her sounds with mine, stitch
the tips of consonants into scarves
to tie around our necks, or pull
the illusion of understanding

from behind our ears. Instead,
I said, she said—we repeated
the questions, the words

elbowing our ribs, the vowels
bruising our cheeks, before
drifting, falling silently
to the vinyl floor.

Prayer for the Exhumation

Cementerio de Cristóbal Colón

"Let Poseidon rise, his waters
pooling off his crown and neck,
rushing down his back and down

his chest and off his hips
until his sea raises its head
and arms over walls and down

streets into this: these sleeping
quarters framed north to south,
east to west, streets crisscrossing,

numbered and mapped, as neatly
laid as our dead, their arms
folded, fingers interlaced—how

we left him. Certain he'd remain
entombed, its bleached stones
warming every knuckle, rib

and tooth, marking his place
in his ruin until someone stole
the plaque, pushed back the slab

and moved him from the grounds
for his ground. My father gone—
for good. Let Poseidon crash

the gates and sink these graves and
immerse whatever still abides,
still lives, deep in a swell

that sloughs the island of its skin,
until land and sea become one.
Let fish feed along cobbled roads,

dart through arches and gates
as if coral reefs; let whales breed
near domes and birds alight

on the tips of steeples and crosses;
let the horizon collapse
into the murky water, the clear blue

lost to silt and turmoil, as lost
as my father. And years from now,
if the sea recedes and walls dry

and the first palms seed,
let someone find the city
and honor the remains,

all who were, all who called this
home, so our mourning can end,
so, together, we might begin again."

Offering

The cat in her shedding winter coat
prances, meaning she has broken
the neck of an unsuspecting mouse
and laid it on the old brick patio
in my lover's yard. She howls
until we rise and step out into
spring air, saying, *Good. Good Bear.*
At times she shows her teeth
before dropping down, exposing
her side, and why not?
Who hasn't destroyed out of love,
then asked to be forgiven?

Paradise Island

after Wonder Woman

If you choose to leave, the mother says
as her daughter sets sail,
you may never return. They face
different shores, the light
a darkness that strains. Everything
hued blue, the near-bronze
of tarnished shields.

No angel hovers above.
And the gate she passes through is
simply a shimmer. I can't recollect
what happens next,
only *Who will I be if I stay?*

and the mother growing smaller,
first a figure, then a fist, then
an imagined speck where land
is indistinguishable from sea.

First Year Gone

In the dark, I untie the knots, my fingers
loosening each familiar row.

I've come to think of this unloosening
as stilling time, as undoing change,
but still, time pools light. No matter
how much I unravel, light pools and you—
you remain as far now as you were
when I first knit these rows.

This morning I drape the shapeless garment
over my head like a mourning veil,
the woolen veil heavy,
woolen yarn pilose from the
knotting, unknotting, its fibers
scratching my lips. You've become
a dream, my lips tasting only
damp wool, an ocean bed
drained of seawater, its kelp
drying in summer heat—if only I could
cross the dry basin
before storms flood the ocean once more.

To the Stranger Up North

I'll never fit between your palms.
Go ahead, see me as the dying galaxy
your telescope seeks, your one eye
closed so all's gas and loss. I'm close,
but ninety miles can take days to cross
and water's hungrier than sharks.
My people leave, play house
in cities they fill with bodegas
and pastel schools. Their children
speak last century's tongue,
study my curves on maps, and wait
for a border to open like a gate.
What sea respects walls, what walls
break the will of those living
on either side? Tunnel deeper, faster.
Rent a boat, sail closer to shore,
or not. I see you from here:
same storms, same parents
naming their daughters, same families
divided—same gravity, same anger—
each with its own madman
standing on the verandah and waving
his power like a child's toy.

Navigation

By New Year's, I dye a tennis ball red
and name it Mars like science kids
rigging a solar system from hangers
and string. By March, the snowplows
in ditches, house dirty, kitchen
faucet broken, I bounce Mars
under the bed and call it a dust storm.
I dream of living in a spacecraft—
seven months of cramped muscles
and silent meals. Avalanches billowing
rust red. Craters filled with red ice.
Air too thin to breathe, a year
shaped by too many losses. I hang
my body over the bed's edge and feel
the new ground with hands clumsy
in spacesuit gloves, and reach-reach-
reach into the darkness until it is almost
more than my body can bear.

The Players

They're at it again—the back and back and back,
heat lamps and bonfire breaking the darkness,

their paddled hands reaching to pull the ball
back to the table, back to each other. They bend

and brace their legs, withdraw, then lunge close.
Nightly I watch them from my kitchen, though

the small white ball is impossible to see
in the snow filling the yards between us.

Between the seeing and not being seen,
the ball hovers, a trick of light, maybe,

a lack of certainty before it snaps clear
like a lost lover glimpsed at the deli counter,

how the profile you once knew intimately
can startle you—its sudden appearance.

Two men still play under a tarp
as the snow thickens, the night darkens:

Now the slap of paddle against ball, the *thunk*
of ball on table, the air growing colder and farther

between them, between us, until sight dissolves
in the snowstorm, leaves me listening

when the ball shoots off the side,
when they submit and return inside.

Gemini, the Moon Welcomes You

Tonight the moon is a motel sign welcoming you home.

Tonight you appear above, twin figures on a distant shore,
      oily black, not unlike the canals we once bobbed in.

To keep me from drowning, you'd said the water reached
      miles and miles and miles before touching the silky
      bottom. A child, I floated close, afraid anything lost
      would sink in darkness.

Tonight I stand in a field, trace each one of your stars: head
      to heart to limb, but one hand fades in the watery
      sky, and the other drifts—a plane, slow-going.

I'm forgetting. The map to reach you pale and wordless.

IV.

Legend

During the war, women hid messages
  inside white flowers
tucked in their hair. They crossed
  enemy lines, slipped the blossoms
into soldiers' fists. What might
  win the war: a child's crown
for her communion, an offering
  at a grave. The ovule,
the style, the stigma—what seemed
  to unfurl overnight took weeks,
even years. Dream your hand
  plucks the bloom, its widest
petals like porcelain, and a halo
  of bees skims your arms.
Upon waking, walk to the docks,
  the bloom heavy behind your ear,
and breathe in its sweet persistence,
  its scent of sea salt and gutted fish.

After Exile

The bird refused to eat
after my sister fled.

Its slack beak chewed air
then clacked shut as if cracking
a seed. Yet when offered fruit,
it flapped and bit my cupped hand.

Who was I to that bird?

It understood longing hungers longer
than anyone could hold out
their hand.

Incantation

Not even flight patterns offer certainty tonight.
Which words will bring you beside me tonight?

The plane trembles over your state line. Mountains,
plains—how do I map our geography tonight?

Rain ferries across your streets, inverts the stars.
Nearly asleep, I know snow muffles my eaves tonight.

Once, we lived together—our time marked
by a season, a plan. Why think of that lease tonight?

Extrañar, to miss, as in, *extraño tu voz en la mañana,*
Me extraña as in, how odd your voice feels tonight.

You say planes are also arrivals. Why is there always
a suitcase half-packed? Forgive my defeat tonight.

These nights, these archipelagos of words:
Say *skin, breath, tongue*—say *Helena, here, tonight.*

A Question on Symbolism

Does language cry out,
its voice an island shrinking
as the plane pulls away?

        "Don't be so dramatic," she says
        over the phone.

Syllables tamped by engine whirs,
the words indecipherable?

        Onions falter, grease snaps.
        "Listen—

Does each accent sound of knots
pulled taut, or does language
ribbon a waist, hold who she was?

        A bird is still a bird,
        whatever you call it."

What knee does one kneel and
pray upon? What does one say?
What ritual soothes the ear
mourning what's lost?

        The knife thuds the cutting board,
        a final word—

I stutter, words

           a comfort

I cannot find,

          she cannot offer.

Bozza Imperfetta of Sight

The tourists arrive. Dogs roam, smaller than the strays
back home, then sleep, teats exposed, on warm stone
roads. The tourists snap pictures; they snap pictures of
each other snapping pictures; as expected, they snap
pictures of cars—a 1950s Ferrari, a red taxi with Rubenesque
curves. Strangers wave, pose: A man palms a blue cake,
another grips a chicken by its feet, its wings twitching. At
a cathedral, the tourists enter without genuflecting; they
enter reflections, each a prayer gracing the tile floors, the
faces of the faithful. The tourists study their maps.

The tourists crowd a van, drive to the countryside. There
they break bread with the people—fried plantains, ropa
vieja, wine. Half-hunched, a man beats time with his cane—
he calls the host by name, he sings: *I've seen your wife*,
sings: *she's climbed into my bed*. The tourists look from man
to man.

Back in the city, the tourists stroll the promenade. An
arched window opens nowhere. A wall salutes the street,
its scaffolding woven with weeds and vines. Farther
down, boys play soccer under a stairway floating midair.
Each step climbs and climbs, never arriving.

Equinox

for Manuela

On the doorstep, the brown package waited. The hand
    that printed my address could have been yours.

Unexpected, like a memory returning so quickly the air
    filled with chamomile tea, and then suddenly gone.

Inside, avocados shifted: two, maybe three—green against
    newsprint, against an inside out grocery bag,
    its letters inversed.

I didn't sleep that night. The green shone too bright.

In the movie, the protagonist wouldn't look anyone in the
    eye when she spoke. As if turning away freed her.

Morning crackles more clearly through the trees.

Waiting to Meet in San Francisco

Two hawks—one dives
behind the skyline, loops back
to brush the other's
soft chest, then grips.
As one they plummet.
Say the sky is a swooping arm.
Say the city's clangs and lights
will buoy their frames.
Say that one will release the other
before street glass dazzles them
senseless. Say yes. Say you will
let go, say you'll never,
say air will catch us both.

Restoration

1.

Yes, an island caught in time—you'd heard
stories, read books, thought you knew

what to expect. You packed clothes, food,
medicine, perfume—what others might need.

Now, in a cramped hotel room, you unlock
the suitcase, your second cousins nodding

thank you, thank you. Nod despite your fear,
the food isn't enough. Outside, the walls

shed skin like sunburnt girls, buildings stand
with three sides, balconies threaten to fall.

You travel from cemetery to church,
wander street to street, plaza to plaza,

and snap shots of a saint missing its head,
a burnt-out church, a monument of feet,

its body lost to rebellion. You unfold
the map, refold the map. You open

the guidebook, its photos matte and dated,
its pages smooth, its type small and finite.

2.

Dream the city is on fire, inhale its heat,

its sooty blackness. Wake, breathless,

the sun browning your face. Rise,

walk through the city of ruin. Someone

asks for milk, asks for bread, asks…

Peer through broken windows, glimpse

a hand cupping a mouth. Is it a hand

holding laughter, or a hand holding back

whatever needs to be said? Understand

the story about fish and loaves

leavened from a basket to feed thousands

is not about faith but about hunger.

3.

Flamboyan petals beckon and burn.
Let your eyes look, they will not
deceive. They see beyond

what you thought, they see
without reason.

Taste flowers, bitter red.
Sweet rum, the hint of mint. Your skin
tastes of salt, of diesel engines,
of lemons. Ice cubes chill your teeth,
a moment of sharp pain, until

laughter unrolls from someone's tongue,
its sound a joy that could
topple the houses around you.

Here Is Born from There

A Havana bed where she woke
and dreamt *there*, a place
without army-green
and camo fatigue, a city
aching in whiteness, snow
splitting acres into years.
I want to see my mother
eat chocolate before breakfast
small bits stuck to her teeth,
hair pinned up, face aging,
her house humid, mine stale
like air in unused suitcases.
The space between *there*
and *here*—doesn't it nestle,
one inside the other,
a *t* the only thing keeping us
apart as we sip tea?
Our neon sun, its light,
reaches us faster than we
could reach it, an eon
of too-bright distance that, I wish,
I could arrange
and rearrange into *none*,
into *no, no one*—if I cheat,
or *not one*—if I borrow,
as in, *not one more day*,
as in, this is the year

we remove *t*
from every phrase we speak:
Here — savor a milky square.
Know neon is only a color
for home, *for* love, *for* now.

In Defense of Orpheus

That cold afternoon in the cemetery:
a blue flash, both of us turning and pointing
at the passing swallow—like that,

or like turning toward your stillness,
asleep before the television, so ordinary
after months measuring our distance

by hours, as a darkness not unlike
a planetarium, the dome speckled above,
so the Milky Way seemed more attainable

than us. That impulse. To turn and reach
for your hand, even when the story
reminds me I could lose you, and nothing

would bring you home. Still, I will turn—
whatever light or darkness might befall us.

Home, First Winter

I expected a fist of steel mills
puffing soot. A grid of icy streets
luging into a mountainside.
Damn if your river's too
toxic to touch, your winter
a dusk that never ends,
your roads wending and
wending. This, all of
this—my calves sore
from walking up hill
after hill. My back sore
shoveling snow and falling
as I salt. The drive-thru
voice spitting, *I can't
understand you*. What could I
have expected? Not tunnels
that open out of darkness
into a bridge so full of light
I wanted to sing
church hymns. Your spring
the hue of hydrangea
bluing again, their small eyelids
shivering. Or the lilies
tangled in their wild joy.

Prayer for No Country

Between my want   and your want

for me, I envision our universe:

a kerchief, each tip   gently pulled to

       its fuchsia center,

the cloth creased. And ironed.

You will turn over the new square,

and repeat.   My turn, your turn—

and repeat, until   we can no longer

fold the cotton.

Then, you and I

will occupy   not a country

but a hard origami knot,   each part

of us   pressed against

the other.

Acknowledgments

The Adroit Journal: "Duende with Poppies"

Arts & Letters: "A Conversation," "Self-Portrait with a Cubano de Paso"

Beloit Poetry Journal: "The Lesson"

Dialogist: "Home, First Winter"

The Florida Review: "Here Is Born from There"

Four Way Review: "Bozza Imperfetta of Sight," "Prayer for No Country"

Ilanot Review: "Paradise Island"

The Inflectionist Review: "First Year Gone," "A Question on Symbolism"

The Los Angeles Review: "Love Letter to a Stranger, with Rain," "To the Stranger Up North," "The Visit"

ONE ART: "For the First Girl I Loved"

Pleiades: "The Body Is Not a Stone"

Poem-a-Day: "Legend"

Poet Lore: "Offering," "The Players"

Prairie Schooner: "Prayer for the Exhumation," "Restoration," "609 Delicias Street, La Víbora, La Habana, Cuba"

Puerto del Sol: "Ineffable," "There"

RHINO: "Against Paradise"

Rogue Agent: "Our Bodies Stood Like Houses"

The Shore: "Late"

Southern Humanities Review: "The want for faith"

Sou'wester: "On Love"

SWWIM Every Day: "Incantation"

"The Lesson" was featured on *Verse Daily* on May 24, 2019.

For their guidance and support, heartfelt thanks to Blas Falconer, Laurie Posner, and Shannon K. Winston—they generously read draft after draft, helped shape this book, and sustained me. Special thanks to Danit Brown, Anne McCauley, and Ashley Miller for their constant encouragement and rich conversations about poetry, writing, and the creative process. Thanks to Eavan Boland, Grace Li, Silvina López Medin, Tyler Mills, and Nancy Pearson for their inspiring workshops, as well as Maggie Smith for her thoughtful edits.

Thanks to the friends who offered conversation, laughter, and inspiration—Holger Elischberger, Veronica Golos, Karen Harryman, Vandana Khanna, Beth Martinelli, Scott

Melzer, Brian Smith, Amy Terstriep, and Lynn Verduzco-Baker. Thanks to the Community of Writers, The Hambidge Center for the Creative Arts, and the Virginia Center for the Creative Arts for offering the space and time to begin many of these poems. Thanks to Albion College for the Hewlett-Mellon Fund for Faculty Development grants that supported my writing. Thanks to Jorge Mayet for allowing *Demasiado tiempo sin que tu estés* to grace the cover of this collection. Thanks to Diane Lockward—for her insight and her decision to publish this book. Lastly, thanks to my parents and sisters, for their love, for their encouragement.

About the Author

Helena Mesa is the author of *Horse Dance Underwater* (Cleveland State University Poetry Center) and a co-editor of *Mentor and Muse: Essays from Poets to Poets* (Southern Illinois University Press). Her poems have appeared in *Cimarron Review, Indiana Review, Pleiades, Prairie Schooner, Third Coast*, the Academy of American Poets' Poem-a-Day series, and elsewhere. A fellow at the Virginia Center for the Creative Arts and The Hambidge Center for the Creative Arts, she lives in Ann Arbor, Michigan, and teaches at Albion College.

Printed in the USA
CPSIA information can be obtained
at www.ICGtesting.com
LVHW090749140923
756648LV00032B/206